But maybe it wa than you expec

Like many new parents, you might feel excited, proud and happy - but maybe not all the time. With nappies, and crying, 2am feeds, sick on your shoulder, perhaps a partner who doesn't understand or is finding things difficult, or no partner, constant exhaustion, career affected, and perhaps a guilty feeling that you're supposed to be a proud parent who is coping ever so well.

Some parents seem to cope and manage well, whereas most can feel exhausted and sometimes struggle to meet all the demands they face. Some people adjust to their new role as a parent faster than others.

The thing is, what you're feeling isn't unnatural or even unusual. You haven't 'failed' and it doesn't mean you're a bad parent or you've got a difficult baby. It can take time for you and your baby to develop your relationship and relax into your time together.

Instead, it means those fairy tales are exaggerated and you're a lot closer to reality than those film stars who talk about immediate fulfillment and mums who bounce back into their pre-pregnancy clothes within a week or so.

You may be struggling with how you feel and have doubts about your ability to be a good enough parent.

And if you think it would also help to get some sleep, find some energy, stop feeling overwhelmed, rediscover the old you and lay the foundations for a lovely relationship with your baby, you've come to the right book.

So, let's start by working out what makes you feel low, stressed or irritable.

* For ease of writing we have used the word parent throughout. Families come in all sorts of shapes and sizes and this book should be read with this in mind.

3

So, choose a time when you feel worse, then ask...

What's going on?

Lots of things change when you have a baby. Many are positive - perhaps feeling happy and relaxed, loving the hugs, and the joys of having your baby. But at times you may feel exhausted, stressed, down and out of balance in key areas of your life.

These include:

Altered thinking: You want to be positive and in control, but at times it doesn't seem this way and you can feel over-whelmed. Are any of the following familiar?

"There's too much to do."

"I'm so tired I can't cope."

"I'll never get the hang of feeding."

"I'm such a useless parent."

"I don't feel attractive any more."

"Will we have enough money with another mouth to feed?"

"I'm not being allowed to take the time I need off work."

Altered feelings: If you or any partner are stressed you are more likely to be self-critical, and also build worries up in your mind. This may cause you to feel low, stressed, irritable, ashamed or guilty

These strong emotions can have an impact on how you feel physically. Perhaps tiredness creates added pressure between you, your family and friends?

Altered physical symptoms: You and any partner may not be sleeping well. Perhaps there is pain from a C-section, an episiotomy or a tear that can make you feel even worse. Your breasts may ache, or your nipples feel painful. You feel exhausted, aren't sleeping well, and stress makes you feel even worse.

Altered behaviours: All of these changes can add up to affect what you do. Your new focus on your baby means there's less time to get things done. You may find it harder to do things. You may try and cope by cutting down what you do, trying to make it through. But the less you do, the worse you feel. And the worse you feel, the less you do.

Or sometimes when we feel stressed we go into overdrive and try and do-do-do - when what we need is to slow down and focus on getting a better balance.

And you know what happens then?

YOU CAN FALL INTO A VICIOUS CYCLE

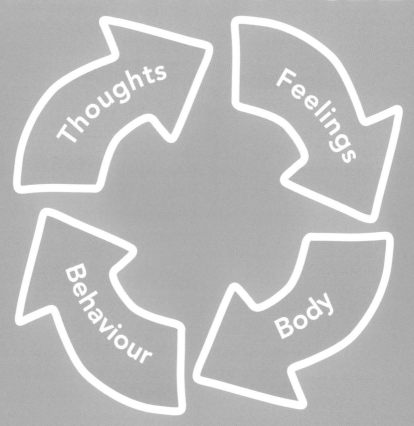

And the cycle can spin, making you feel worse and worse

We've looked at four key areas that can change when you feel under pressure – thinking, emotional and physical feelings and behaviours. There's a fifth area to consider too- the people and events around you. That's the area outside the cycle on the diagram.

What events make you feel worse?

Well it might be your baby waking crying for the fourth time tonight. Or your friend saying "my baby could do this or that by this time." Or "helpful" advice from people, or too much to do, or not enough money.

There may also be other things going on in life like bills to pay, jobs to do, other children, housework, not to mention the pressure of feeling we have to maintain existing relationships and friendships.

And all the demands can build up.

These things outside you can make you feel worse inside too by making the cycle spin.

You may start to change what you do in ways that backfire. Are you pushing people away? Being rude to people who care for you? Or isolating yourself, not asking for the help you need? Perhaps you lean on drink or drugs to cope when you know that's bad for you and your baby?

So...

WHAT ABOUT YOU?

Complete your own five areas assessment

Do you fall into vicious cycles from time to time? Here's how to play detective and work out how the vicious cycle may be affecting you.

Choose two recent times when you felt worse. To start with don't pick times that are really upsetting or too distressing. Instead choose situations when you feel a bit down, fed up, stressed, scared, frustrated, guilty, ashamed, exhausted, or in pain.

Use the next two pages to work out if you have a vicious cycle that is spinning. The good news is the cycle can be made to spin the other way if you know how!

Pen at the ready?

9

Now it's time to spot that vicious cycle

My Five Areas Assessment

What's going on? Describe the situation:

My thoughts.

Thoughts

My behaviour.

Behaviour

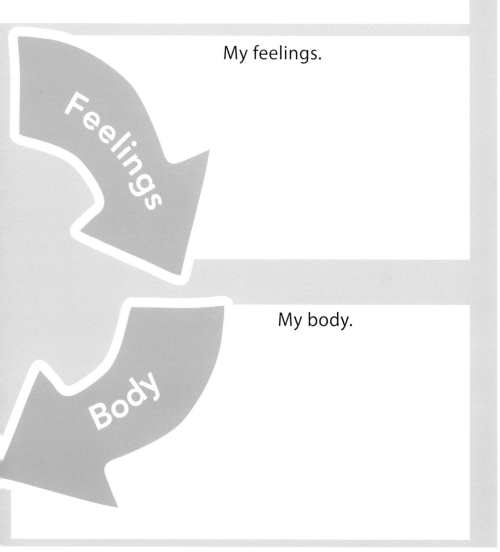

My feelings.

Feelings

My body.

Body

HOW TO CHANGE THINGS AROUND

15 changes to help you feel better

To enjoy this time more, here are 15 changes you can make to your life. There are some things that may be immediately good for building your relationship with your baby, some that are especially good for you, and finally one's that help you change how you respond to others.

You can't make them all at once of course, but if you change one thing at a time, you may feel more content, and so might your baby.

So this is what to do: Every time you turn a couple of pages in this book, we'll suggest one change to your life, your thoughts, your routine, or your relationships. There are 15 changes altogether. These are just ideas to pick and choose from as you find helpful. Plan changes at the speed that works for you and your family.

When you have a moment to yourself, start by making a cup of tea and slowly read through the book at your own pace, thinking about the different changes and scribbling notes in the margins.

There is a section at the end of the book to help you make effective plans to change how things are.

Now, let's find out about one of the first changes you can choose to make.

Turn over for some changes that are good for your baby

13

Discover what sounds make you and your baby smile

Your baby won't yet fully understand what you're saying but they love to hear you saying it. They really like it when you look in their eyes and they think you're fantastic when you pull silly faces and have fun together. Talk gently to them or hum a favourite tune while cuddling them or changing a nappy. That way your baby will learn that you are there, and are interested in them and how they feel. It's all part of building a close bond.

Of course, no-one can cope with goo-goo noises all day long, not you and not your baby, so the best thing is to do it when it feels right for you and your baby. This may be several times a day, and it's helpful getting into a regular routine. There's no such thing as perfect play - just do what you can.

You can do it while changing or bathing, or after a sleep. You can also do it with toys, of course. But don't rush out and empty the toyshop. Banging a spoon on a plastic cup is the baby equivalent of a games console to a teenager! Also, don't underestimate how exciting your face is to your baby. ☺

Sometimes, you may notice your baby looking away from you in the middle of a play session. This isn't boredom, it's thinking. Babies' brains have to take in so much brand new stuff that occasionally, they need a pause to sort it all out.

Here's some ideas of games you can play together:

1. Peek-a-boo.

2. Singing lullabies or nursery rhymes while having hands clapped gently.

3. Banging things to make a noise.

4. Copycat – take it in turns to copy your babies expression, or watch for when they copy you and play along together.

5. Splashing water in the bath.

Make every day an opportunity for fun when you and your baby can really enjoy each other.

Babies need time to stop, think and reflect as they process, discover and learn. Keep things simple and comment on what you see and do together.

Your baby was born loving books

Although babies don't understand words, they understand tones and sounds very well. And when you read a book to your baby, you're sending some of the loveliest sound messages there are.

Face your baby while reading, so that he or she can see your eyes and your expression. Being able to see the book is also a good idea and don't be surprised if your baby reaches out for it.

Reading can be a calming thing to do before bed, but can be a fun thing to do anytime. But don't worry about having to buy a lot of books, there are plenty at the library or charity shop.

Of course, you might think "If my baby doesn't understand words, what's wrong with reading the same book over and over?" There's nothing to stop you doing that, but instead why not give yourself some variety!

Although today may be the first time you try reading to your baby, do think about making it part of the daily routine.

TAKE A BREAK

When you feel stress rising, take a mental step back. Slow things down. Drop your shoulders down (they tend to rise up towards your ears if you get tense). And breathe. Close your mouth and breathe with the lower part of your chest - taking normal size breaths through your nose.

You can get free MP3 relaxation downloads as part of the Living Life to the Full course at www.llttf.com/resources, or use any other relaxation technique that works for you.

... that works for you and your baby

Having to get out of bed to get your baby up, dressed and fed can be a struggle, especially on cold mornings when you haven't slept much. But having a routine can really help.

As long as your baby is comfortable, get yourself up and get washed and dressed when you have time. Routines can help because they give you a structure to the day. But be flexible if you need to, and do these at a time that works for you. After your baby and you are up, then make yourself a routine with other things. Maybe make a pot of coffee. Or listen to the radio. Maybe doing some tidying, popping to the corner shop to say hello and buy some fruit, or phoning a friend. Perhaps walking in the park with the pram with friends.

It helps to have a daily routine that can flexibly fit in with your baby's needs.

It must also contain more than chores. That walk, that sit down with the radio or a book, time on social media, connecting with someone online, having a chat, that phone call with your parents or a friend – they're all as important as the washing up (actually, they're more important).

So sit and think what might be helpful to put in your diary this week. If it's helpful, you can use the *Activity Planner* over the page to plan your days from now on.

My activity planner

Plan a balance of activities over the days and week. Choose things you value and give a sense of pleasure and achievement or help you spend time with people you like.

Build things up over a few weeks, perhaps aiming for one activity planned in each part of the day. It might be something you do with your baby, or with a partner, friend of family member. Leave some gaps for the unexpected things that crop up. When you can, don't forget to also plan some time just for you.

Try to get into a routine- a time to get up, eat, go to bed, and do the household chores, or perhaps to go for a walk, meet friends or attend a regular class. Over time, your plan might include returning to work if you are on maternity or paternity leave.

Plan in the key essentials that otherwise will build up and cause you problems- paying bills, cutting the lawn, doing the washing up, ironing, having a hair cut etc.

living
life to
the full
www.llttf.com

My Activity Planner

	Morning	Afternoon	Evening
Monday			
Tuesday			
Wednesday			
Thursday			

	Morning	Afternoon	Evening
Friday			
Saturday			
Sunday			

NOW HERE ARE SOME THINGS TO ADD INTO YOUR ACTIVITY PLANNER

Work out what makes you feel good

Write down some things you've enjoyed, have given you a sense of pleasure or achievement, or helped you feel close to someone. Again think broadly, so you include time with your baby, any partner, family or friends, or things just for you.

Things I have enjoyed:

_____

_____

Things I've done/achieved:

_____

_____

Things that make me feel close to others:

_____

_____

What about essential activities that you need to do like paying bills?

_____

_____

Pick activities that make you feel good, and start to plan them into the *Activity Planner* across the days and week.

Next, you're going to build on these activities

25

Next, try to re-connect with people. Even if you don't feel like it

We often avoid people when we're feeling down. We can be bound up with our own troubles and sometimes can't be bothered getting out of the house to talk to anyone else. Even phoning a friend can seem too hard to do.

But loneliness just makes anyone feel worse and worse, so if you feel like this, you could try out the following ideas over time.

Maybe phone a friend and ask if you can come round with your baby. See if they are free to meet online or face to face later today, or arrange to meet another time.

Also, think whether it might be helpful to find out what local parent and baby groups and classes are available near you.

Consider whether you want to try and broaden your circle of friends, or whether you are happy with your existing friendship group. Meeting others can be good for you and also great for your baby.

26

Why not go for a walk today?

People who recover from really bad times often say they appreciate things they used to take for granted. So get your coat on and your baby all wrapped up and take a walk. Go see the world for the amazing place that it is.

Even better, do it with a friend or your partner if you have one. Try and walk somewhere pretty or interesting. Or change your route regularly so there's variety and always something to talk about.

While you're walking, really notice what's around you. The wind, the warmth, the cold, the trees, the flowers, the shops and the sky. Pretend you're seeing them for the first time, like your baby. It can be nice to point things out as you walk if you feel able. He or she won't have the faintest idea what you're saying to start with, but you'll both feel closer and happier. Your voice is the best noise on earth, remember? Some prams allow you to have your baby face you as you walk. Your baby will love that as you're the most exciting thing in the world to them just now.

Time for you

Plan some time to be good to yourself

Choose something that you enjoy. Maybe read a book or go to your favourite social media site, or get a takeaway. You could watch a gripping box-set. You'll feel so much better and your baby will notice that you're happier and more relaxed.

Maybe plan this time when you think it's likely your baby is asleep, or at nursery or with a friend of relative.

Or get your friends round for a bite to eat, a cup of tea, a pamper session or to watch the big match - whatever works for you and your family.

28

Have some *You Time*

Taking some time for yourself for an hour or so is a good way to get life back into perspective. And when you make it a regular session, it becomes something you can really look forward to. Of course, you may need to keep it short at first, especially if you are arranging it around your baby's feeding routine. But as you and your baby (and your babysitter) get into the routine, you could stretch to longer periods.

There's just one idea you might want to stick to - go somewhere or do something that you or both of you want to do. No duty visits to relatives as your only trips out. You time also isn't about catching up on errands or food shopping. Other times are for those things you need to do.

Window shop for clothes or gadgets - whatever takes your fancy. You could see an old friend, watch sport, walk in the park, go to the pictures or the library, treat yourself to tea and a cake with a friend or friends.

If you feel a bit guilty at first, or miss your baby, this is natural as a new parent. For most people this will ease as you start to enjoy your trips.

Time for you moments are really important because they help you to balance things. They are also good for your baby as they start to get used to and know other adults. Make sure you pop it in your phone calendar as a reminder at least once a week from now on.

Some tips on staying happy

Doing things that give you a sense of pleasure or achievement, and help you spend time with people you like can help improve how you feel. There are also plenty of other things you can do that will help to keep your spirits up.

You could choose activities that help you get fitter as well as happier. Here are some ideas:

Happy Steps

Exercise is good for you. So good that when you do it, your body says 'thanks' by sending happy chemicals to your brain. But not everyone has the time or money to go to the gym.

If you are out and about without the pram, use the stairs as often as you can, whether you are at home, or out and about. Take the opportunity and include slopes and small hills in your walks pushing the pram or buggy. Getting your heart beating faster is one of the best ways to get fitter and make you feel better in yourself too.

You could decide to do it next time you're out. Then decide to keep on doing it and always take the stairs.

Make a Note of This

Music cheers you up. Obvious? So why are you sitting there in silence if you find silence is just a space for you to think about your worries in?

You could try putting some of your favourite music on. Why not try it now? Play music while you're bathing your baby or doing the dishes. Play music while you're walking briskly to the shops. Play music while you're sitting around.

It might be best not to play sad music, or songs that remind you of unhappy times. Keep it upbeat and you'll get an instant lift.

Take One Away

When you're feeling under pressure, it's tempting to reach for the phone or online menu and have food delivered. But eating too much fast food or takeaway food is a great way to get really down.

Did you see that experiment where someone ate nothing but fast food? They felt depressed and really unhealthy within a couple of weeks.

So here's what you do: cut out one take-away a week. Just one. Replace it with something you make yourself (whatever is easy for you).

Within just a week or so, you may notice you feel lighter, fitter and happier. And a bit better off.

Time to remember the good times

When you're down it's easy to forget the good times. The times you've succeeded in something, happy times with your baby, family and friends, things that make you smile.

So each evening, why not sit down and write down some of the things that you:

- **have enjoyed**

- **felt was a job well done**

- **or helped you feel close to someone else**

After a few days, you'll have a list of great things that you can look back on, and this will help you feel a lot better.

living
life to
the full
www.llttf.com

My Happy List

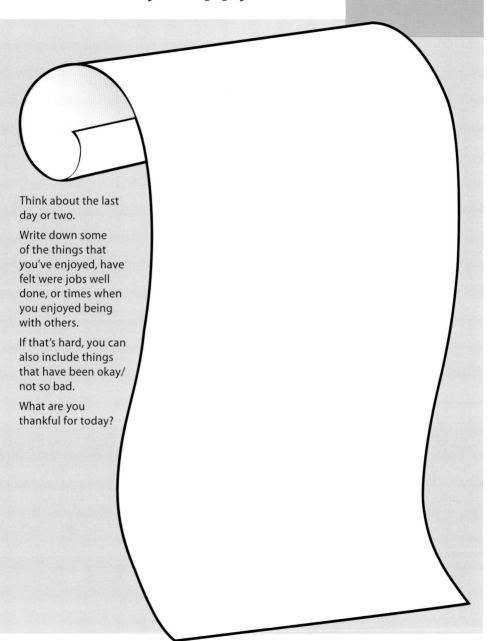

Think about the last day or two.

Write down some of the things that you've enjoyed, have felt were jobs well done, or times when you enjoyed being with others.

If that's hard, you can also include things that have been okay/ not so bad.

What are you thankful for today?

When you're upset, it's time to work out what is going on

When you're feeling low, the way you think can make you feel even worse. You may beat yourself up for not being a good parent or for leaving the housework. Maybe you assume others think badly of you, or perhaps you take responsibility for everything.

From now on, we're going to call all these things 'Unhelpful Thoughts'. Because they're not helpful, they're usually not true and they make you feel bad emotionally, and can affect what you do in ways that make things even worse.

So think back over some times when you've felt worse. Low, stressed, angry, guilty or ashamed. Or perhaps exhausted or unable to cope.

What went through your mind at the time?

About what you've done or not done?

About you?

About others?

About what has happened?

About what might happen?

About what others think about you?

Any pictures or images that come into your mind?

Now fill in the little chart on the next page and tick the kind of unhelpful thoughts that you noticed then.

Are you your own worst critic?
Do you always seem to be beating yourself up about something?

Do you focus on the bad stuff?
As if you were looking at the world through darkened glasses?

Do you have a gloomy view of the future?
Expecting everything to turn out badly.

Are you jumping to the worst conclusions?
It's called 'catastrophising'.

Do you assume that others see you badly?
When you haven't checked whether it's true, it's called 'mind-reading'.

Do you take responsibility for everything?
Including things that aren't your fault.

Are you always saying things like 'Should' 'Ought to' 'Got to'?
Setting impossible standards for yourself?

Trying not to think about it doesn't work

Did you know that trying not to think about something that is upsetting, tends to bring it on even more than before? So, if I was to ask you to try really hard not to think about a white polar bear, you might be able to do it by maybe deliberately thinking about a green polar bear instead for a short time. Perhaps you could keep it up for 10 seconds, or ten minutes - but could you keep it up for 10 hours or 10 days? It would be an impossible task. Trying hard not to think about something isn't a very effective solution.

Fortunately experts in psychological research have discovered there are some far more effective ways of dealing with unhelpful thinking than trying not to think about it.

Turn the page to find out more

The Amazing Unhelpful Thought Busting Programme (AUTBP) is a great way to respond when unhelpful thoughts crowd into our mind and make us feel more and more upset.

1. Label the thought

When you notice one of those unhelpful thoughts, mentally step back and stick a label on it. "Oh, that's just one of those unhelpful thoughts".

When you label an upsetting thought this way, it loses its power and you realise that it's just part of being upset. It's not the truth, it's just one of those unhelpful thoughts. That's something you practiced in Change 10: Play thought detective.

2. Now leave it alone

Move the focus of your attention away from the unhelpful thought. Don't challenge it or try to argue with it, just let it be. An unhelpful thought loves attention, so don't give it any.

Instead, think about what you're doing right now, or focus right down onto what's happening just now, your breathing, the touch of your baby's hand, or smell of their head after a bath. Or choose to recall your plans for the future, or things you've achieved lately.

3. Stand up to it!

Unhelpful thoughts are like bullies. They say you won't like doing something. They say you'll fail if you try. They tell you you're useless or you're scared or nobody likes you.

But this is just a thought, not the truth. Don't be bullied! Act against it and test it out! If the thought says "Don't" then DO! If the thought says "Can't" say "CAN!" right back at it.

4. Give yourself a break

Unhelpful thoughts are how we beat ourselves up when we're upset. So if you're having trouble with an unhelpful thought, think what the person who loves you most in the world would say.

What words of encouragement and support might they offer? They'd disagree with the upsetting thoughts, wouldn't they? They'd remind you that you're great and most certainly not a failure or a poor parent.

Trust these compassionate words and let them help you get rid of the unhelpful thoughts.

5. Look at it differently

Some unhelpful thoughts keep coming back and you wonder if you'll ever get the better of them. Here are some things you can do that can help.

Give yourself some good advice

Imagine what it would be like if it was a friend, not you, who was having this unhelpful thought. What advice would you give? Now give the same advice to yourself. Do you apply one set of standards to yourself and a different one to others?

Put your thought or worry into perspective

Does it really matter so much? Will it matter in six days, six weeks or six months? Will you even remember what the problem was? If it won't matter over time, it's probably not that important now!

How would others deal with the problem?

Think about someone who seems to handle problems well and work out what they would do, or how they would think in this situation?

Think about the facts, not your feelings

Sometimes we can think unhelpful things because we're feeling low or stressed. Then those thoughts make us feel even worse. If so, try to look past the upsetting thoughts and get to the truth.

living
life to
the full
www.llttf.com

The Amazing Unhelpful Thought Busting Programme

Try the Amazing Unhelpful Thought Busting Programme (AUTBP) - for unhelpful thoughts that have a bad impact on how you feel emotionally or physically, or on what you do.

1 Label it
- Oh, you're just one of those unhelpful thoughts.

2 Leave it
- Unhelpful thoughts often demand attention. Let them be.

3 Stand up to it
- Unhelpful thoughts can be intimidating. You can beat them.

4 Be kind to yourself: Give yourself a break

- What warm words of encouragement would someone say?
Say them to yourself.

5 Look at it differently

- Give yourself the advice you'd give a friend.

- Ask yourself if it will matter in six weeks or months?

- What would other people you trust and respect say?

- Does it really matter so much?

- Are you looking at the whole picture?

You're not going to sleep like a baby

But these simple rules can help you have a better night

It may take you and your baby quite some time to get into a feeding/sleeping routine. So the best thing to do in that time is help the process along by starting each day around the same time and trying to feed and change them at regular intervals.

Take your own naps when you can and, of course, get friends and partners to help with the housework etc.

As things start to settle down, you may find you start to have more time for sleep. So here are some ideas that you can use to build into a regular sleep routine.

These things work

Both your baby and you can benefit from a wind-down period before bed. Bathing your baby can become part of a routine that leads on to sleep. You can use the same principles of a wind-down period yourself. Have a bath or shower. Focus on calm activities, and if you find you can't sleep, get up for a short time until you feel sleepy tired - then go back to bed.

Although in general it's best not to nap during the day, you may find early on after your baby is born that you need to take sleep and naps when you can.

It's best for your baby if their bedroom is cosy but not overly warm. Ask your health visitor about the best ways to help your baby fall asleep, and also stay safe in his/her cot or pram.

These don't

Exercise is a bad idea just before bed. Getting physically tired might seem OK, but actually, it's not as good as slowly winding down. Don't do anything strenuous near bedtime.

Avoid caffeine in the hours before sleep. Mute or turn off your mobile phone or switch to airplane mode. Don't smoke either. Smoking wakes you up and smoky air is bad for your baby. If you have to, have your last cigarette half an hour before your bath and smoke in a different room from your baby, or even better outside only.

TV is also a no-no. Watch it to calm down before your bath but get rid of the TV in your bedroom. Lose the radio too, or at least, don't listen to it before sleeping.

If you are breast or chest feeding it's best to avoid alcohol if you can. Speak to your health visitor if you have any questions, but if you choose to drink, it's better to have no more than one or two units of alcohol, just once or twice a week.
(Reference www.nct.org.uk).

Here's some ways to become more assertive

Being assertive isn't the same as being demanding, rude or aggressive. It's simply having the confidence and self-respect to tell others what you need and how you feel, and to say no – quietly but firmly – when you can't go along with something.

It takes practice to be assertive, especially if you've spent years avoiding confrontation and putting other people's needs before your own. But it can be done and there are a couple of simple techniques you can try straight away.

Put it on repeat

If you find yourself in a situation where people want you to do something you don't want to do, you need to simply repeat variations of the same sentence again and again if they keep on asking.

For example: *"That's not going to work for me"* or *"I just can't do that this week"*, or *"I'm sorry I can't do that today"*.

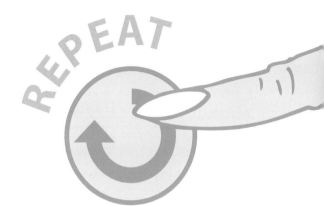

When you've learned your 'lines', simply keep on returning to them throughout the conversation, stating your wishes clearly and calmly until you get your message across.

Saying 'no'

You may think saying 'no' will upset people or make them not like you, but the opposite is often true if you say it the right way – calmly and firmly, and repeating it, like the *Put it on repeat* method above.

Why not try it now? *"No. I won't be able to do that today."* *"No, I have other things to see to at the moment."*

Start to use this important little word and you'll be surprised what a difference it can make.

Now turn the page. We're going to read you your rights…

45

living life to the full
www.llttf.com

The 12 Rules of Assertiveness

I have the right to:

I have the right to:		Plan to do more of this
Respect myself	Who I am and what I do	
Recognise my own needs as an individual	Separate from what's expected of me as a parent, child, friend, partner, colleague - or linked to your role at work or elsewhere etc.	
Make clear 'I' statements about how I feel and what I think	For example 'I feel uncomfortable with your decision'	
Allow myself to make mistakes	It's normal	
Change my mind	If I choose to	
Ask for 'thinking about it' time	When people ask you to do something, you have the right to say 'I'd like to think it over. I'll let you know by the end of the week.'	

Allow myself to enjoy my successes	Being pleased with what I've done and sharing it with others	
Ask for what I want,	Rather than hoping someone will notice what I want	
Recognise that I am not responsible for the behaviour of other adults	Or for pleasing other people all the time	
Respect other people	And their right to be assertive and expect the same in return	
Say 'I don't understand'	So you make sure you work out what is happening	
Deal with others	Without depending on them for approval	

Change 14: 1, 2, 3 breathe

Here's how to change direction if you start to lose your temper

Everyone gets irritable from time to time, but if you find yourself flying off the handle too often, here's a system that really works.

It's all about understanding what pushes your buttons, so you can change how you react in tense situations. We call it the *1,2,3, Breathe!* method.

1. Know your buttons

Think about what makes you lose it. Maybe when you feel unsupported? Or when you're faced by too many demands? Or perhaps when your baby has colic and just can't settle late into the night and you feel you can't cope any more? Know your buttons and you can keep them from being pressed.

Take a few minutes and write your buttons here.

2. Know your early warning system

You feel different just before you snap. With some people it's heavy breathing. Others clench their fists or feel tears welling up. Or maybe your early warnings are in your mind. You start to feel critical of someone else. You don't think much of their voice, their opinions. Maybe you feel ignored or think people are looking down on you?

3. Know your escape hatches - where you respond differently

An escape hatch gets you out of a bad situation. You might just walk away, or pause and count to 10. Other people hum a little tune (music from your favourite film maybe?). When you know a few escape hatches, you can stay in control whatever happens. Here are some ideas:

Smile.

When your face or fists are tensing up, make yourself give out a proper big smile that lights up your face. Others will notice, and it can help things calm down.

Relax your shoulders.

Notice where your shoulders are and make a point of relaxing and letting them drop while you slow down your breathing.

Sit down.

It's a lot harder to explode when you're sitting down, so when you get an early warning, stay in your seat, or go find one.

NOW Breathe!

Drop your shoulders, close your mouth and breathe normal sized breaths at a normal pace.

Change 15: How to fix almost everything

Time to sort things out

When things mount up, they get you down. Piles of ironing or unpaid bills often add to feelings of pressure.

Although it might be hard to face things when they mount up, sorting them out can really lift your mood.

So, when problems occur with the people and events around you, it might be helpful to think how to tackle them.

But where do you start?

Use the Easy 4 Step Plan to make your changes

Changing things in your life is never easy, especially big or complicated things, so here is a system that can handle almost anything.

Choose a problem to work on. Before you start, if you're facing lots of problems, pick just one to work on first.

Next, the Easy 4 Step Plan helps you break things down so that you can really get them done and, as you may have guessed, has four simple steps.

1. Break the problem into chunks

It can be hard to change what you do. So, if you want to start something new, or stop something that's proving unhelpful, the answer is to break it into easy chunks.

Let's say you want to get out of the house with your baby more than you have been, and you could start by planning to get out tomorrow as a first step.

Or if you want to cut down smoking, you could break the week into bits and decide to cut it down on Mondays to start with.

Or you want to reduce the amount of tasks you are trying to fit in each day, use the Activity Planner on pages 22/23 to balance your weekly activities.

Most problems can be chopped up like this, and you're much more likely to succeed when you do things bit by bit.

2. Think of creative ways to tackle the first step

Grab a piece of paper and write down all the things you could do to work on the first bit of the problem.

If you're working on getting out of the house, you might buy a book on trees and try and spot four new types every day as you walk with your baby through the park (explaining about the different leaves in a loud, friendly voice).

Trying to cut down online shopping? Use the parental controls in your browser to lock yourself out of whatever sites you spend money on.

The trick with being creative is to let your mind go, and write everything down - the wacky things as well as the sensible ones.

Do this and there's bound to be a good idea in there somewhere.

3. Choose an idea and make a plan to do it

Look at your creative ideas and pick one. Choose one that looks do-able and doesn't scare you too much.

Now take another piece of paper and write down, step by step, how to actually DO it.

Make the steps as small as you like: Get up. Get dressed. Get your baby ready. Walk to the front door. Open the door....and so on.

Make sure that the steps are small, straightforward and seem like things you could really do.

4. Check the plan and put it into action

This is it! You've written down all the steps, now you need to check that they're do-able. Use this checklist:

Are you aiming at just one thing?

Don't try and do more than one item on your list. You can always pick another when you've sorted the first one.

Is it realistic?

You're not planning to run a marathon are you?

Is it slow enough?

There's no need to rush at things. Your plan can take as long as you like, so long as you stick to it, step by step.

Is it easy- not too big?

Make your steps small and easy and you'll be more likely to do them.

Are you ready to unblock it?

Have you thought about what could go wrong and how to deal with it?

Five ticks?
Then *Go For It!*

PLAN, DO AND REVIEW

Make changes one step at a time

OK. You've read about all the 15 changes that you can make, perhaps scribbled notes in the margins and maybe thought about what you might like to do first. Now its time to choose what you are going to put into practice and start feeling better.

If you are ready, it's time to start planning *what* you are going to do, and *when* you're going to do each change, and in what order.

The *Planner sheet* on the next two pages is designed to help you make an effective plan. Sometimes it can be helpful to get someone involved to give you support with this.

Then use the *Review sheet* on the pages that follow to learn from what happens. Again, you may find it helpful to talk through how things went with someone you trust.

Use them to make better and better plans. Try to get into a cycle of *Plan*, *Do* and *Review* to help you move forwards.

Go for it!

Planner Sheet

Make a Plan!

1. What am I going to do?

Just one small thing

2. When am I going to do it?

That way you'll know if you don't do it

3. What problems or difficulties could arise, and how can I overcome them?

4. Is my planned task -

	Yes	No
• Useful for understanding or changing how I am?	☐	☐
• Specific, so that I will know when I have done it?	☐	☐
• Realistic, practical and achievable?	☐	☐

My notes:

living
life to
the full
www.llttf.com

Review Sheet

How did it go? What did you plan to do?

Did you try to do it?   Yes ☐   No ☐

If yes: What went well?

What didn't go so well?

What have you learned from what happened?

How are you going to apply what you have learned?

If no: What stopped you?

External things (other people, work or home issues etc.)

Internal things (forgot, not enough time, put it off, didn't think I could do it, couldn't see the point etc.)

How can you tackle things differently next time?

ASK FOR THE HELP YOU NEED

It's good to talk - to the right person

Although you might want to hide away and 'just get through it', this won't work. You'll feel better sooner if you talk to someone that you trust. However you feel - low, scared or embarrassed, there is help available.

A friend is good. Or a parent, partner, Health Visitor, colleague, counsellor. Do it when you feel ready and able. Open up with someone you trust – someone you may have been shutting out lately.

What to talk about? Talk about yourself. Explain if you're sometimes unhappy, confused, scared, exhausted or irritated.

Ask for help with household chores, feeding or changing your baby, taking over for an hour or so, taking the other kids off your hands for a while, going for a walk with you, or just coming round and listening.

If you're feeling desperate, ring your GP surgery, 111 or 999/emergency services, or go to the local Accident and Emergency department.

The aim of talking is to get support, but you may also get another benefit – talking about problems tends to sort them out in your head. You'll understand things better and get ready for change.

Talking is something you might need to make time for. You could start now and plan to do it as often as you need to.

61

SHOW THIS PART TO THE PEOPLE YOU'RE CLOSE TO

Hi, thanks for reading this!

Your part in my plan includes understanding, listening and some practical stuff.

First, have a look through the rest of the book and get to know the 15 changes. You'll spot that some of them can't be done alone. There's help needed with bathing baby, household chores, baby sitting and going for walks – so get ready to be called on for some of that!

Also, you may need to polish up your listening skills so that you can really help when talking about my/our feelings. Some people may often struggle to discuss their feeling but anyone can feel like this at times.

You may benefit from doing a bit of research too. Reading about becoming a parent or specific issues such as feeding or post-natal depression can be empowering and useful. There are lots of resources online or in your local library. You could try to seek out information endorsed by reputable organisations such as the NHS or major charities.

Supporting someone sounds straightforward, but it isn't always. You may get irritated or frustrated. You may say or do things that you think are helpful, but don't seem to work. It's even possible to make things worse without realising it.

Don't get discouraged though, just turn the page for a quick checklist on the Do's and Don'ts of helping.

This may be helpful

'Being there' for parents in the long term.

Being willing to talk and offer support when needed.

Being happy to help with household and baby chores.

Encouraging parents to ask questions of their health visitor and other experts.

Encouraging parents to try out the 15 changes in this book, and keep using them.

Having a sense of humour and using it to help parents cope.

Staying positive but realistic – things will get better, but there are no quick fixes.

Encouraging parents to seek extra help when it's needed.

Try and encourage someone who is really struggling to reach out for help if they need it. But if you have concerns for the health and wellbeing of a parent or their baby, you may need to alert others such as their health visitor or doctor.

This might not be
(Even though it may be well meant)

Wrapping parents in cotton wool. It's usually not helpful taking over everything.

Repeatedly nagging. Advice is great. Constantly telling parents what to do isn't.

Shouting. If you feel frustrated with the way things are going, imagine how parents feel. Stay calm. Read pages 48 to 49 of this book.

'Being there' too much. Yes, it's possible. If a parent is always on the phone to you or feels that they can't cope without constantly getting reassurance from someone, they may well need wider help with low mood and anxiety.

Being unrealistic. Too many breezy statements like 'you'll be fine – don't worry!' or 'everything will work out!' eventually can make it seem as if you're not taking things seriously.

Forgetting that people are different. The chance to talk about things can help. If a parent wants this, gently encourage them to talk about their feelings and help by listening without immediately offering solutions.

Further information
3 Courses that help to build a secure foundation

Three courses that together cover the formative years of a child's development - helping both the developing child and their parent(s) to enjoy each other. Teaching how to build the relationship and have fun together, coupled with tried and tested strategies based on the cognitive behavioural therapy model.

All available at www.llttf.com

ENJOY YOUR BUMP

Enjoy your Bump. Your relationship with your child starts even before they are born. The course aims to teach how to get prepared emotionally for the birth, build your own resilience and improve your mood.

ENJOY YOUR BABY

Enjoy your Baby. Having a baby can be a joyful but also challenging time for new parents. *Enjoy your Baby* teaches key life skills that can make a difference. Discover why you feel as you do, as well as increase your sense of closeness and fun with your baby.

ENJOY YOUR INFANT

Finally, Enjoy your Infant is designed to help parents in that time when their baby is starting to assert their own views and independence. This online only course aims to help parents learn how to understand their infants (and their own reactions) and respond in ways that help teach your toddler a language for their feelings.